NICOLA HADFIELD'S
BEAUTIFUL HOMES
of South Africa

NICOLA HADFIELD'S
BEAUTIFUL HOMES
of South Africa

PHOTOGRAPHS BY LIEN BOTHA

decorex_{sa}

Contents

Introduction

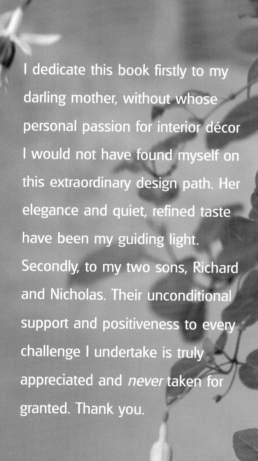

I dedicate this book firstly to my darling mother, without whose personal passion for interior décor I would not have found myself on this extraordinary design path. Her elegance and quiet, refined taste have been my guiding light. Secondly, to my two sons, Richard and Nicholas. Their unconditional support and positiveness to every challenge I undertake is truly appreciated and *never* taken for granted. Thank you.

It was a vulnerable time. When I launched Decorex SA in 1994, things were politically intense in South Africa as nobody seemed to know whether we were in for a peaceful transition or a bloodbath – but as it turned out, it was a hugely positive turning point! It was an enormous relief and there was great joy when our first democratically elected president, Nelson Mandela, was sworn in and, thanks to his extraordinary humility and farsightedness, a gory bloodbath never materialised.

In early January of that year, no company or person, least of all money-lenders, seemed confident to back my idea to showcase our designs on a sophisticated level. I felt that South African interior design was at last 'coming of age' in our country, yet we didn't have a formal platform from which to present … It needed to be world class – up there with the rest of the first world or not at all. My prime intention was to elevate the reputation of our crafts and to present not only to fellow South Africans but also to the outside world what our designs, designers and products were worthy of.

So, with my heart in my mouth, as a single mum of two young boys and despite the capital outlay and a vast savings of R800 – yes, it's true! – I went ahead and prepared for our country's first décor show. The idea paid off, not only personally, but for many others who may never have had the opportunity to get started in their businesses. Our country's first professional design and décor show was conceived as bookings for exhibition space streamed in, bringing wonderful business to many South Africans who, until this stage, had never known success. It is truly thanks to Nelson Mandela, who, by steering a peaceful transition, offered me and many other companies the opportunity to help talented South Africans get started. The rest is happy history. I was bought out some time later by one of the largest conference and event organisers in the world, Rai BV Amsterdam (now known as Thebe Exhibitions), and it was time to move on to new challenges.

With this book, I have tried to follow a similar pattern to that of my design shows, to embrace quality and individuality, and to package both beautifully. During the eight years I was involved with the South African Decorex exhibitions, I found myself in the unique and privileged position of being exposed every year to multiple interpretations of design and style. With this came the enormous pleasure of meeting fascinating and creatively talented people from alternative walks of life. I soon realised that even if, on a purely personal level, I didn't always identify with every style presented, I nevertheless developed a deep appreciation and respect for these designs and the talented individuals who courageously follow their own creative dreams. In my book, most importantly, I wanted to capture the true essence, spirit and soul of each home, its owners and the area in which the house is located.

The ethos of my book

When I came up with the idea of producing a South African-inspired décor book, I wanted to include only private homes, belonging to South Africans, believing this would create an authenticity and ensure a sense of being 'proud to be South African'. By keeping to this formula, it enabled me to promote South African artists, sculptors and craftspeople.

I have intentionally chosen to feature fewer homes (the 'less is more' philosophy!) to give you a genuine feel of the home and the owners' individual creativity and preferred lifestyle choice. I can recognise originality as well as the courage of a person's convictions in making certain design decisions. In this sense it is a very personal book. It is a diverse selection of stylish, characterful homes, all with their own sense of identity and bearing testimony to a truly South African lifestyle. You won't see these homes documented anywhere else, and I have ensured that none is commercially driven. Because of this, I'd like to take the opportunity, right upfront, to thank the owners most sincerely for revealing their hearts and personal lives to me, so that I could bring you a taste of some talented, genuine South Africans. I never imagined that for three years I would be venturing on such an inspirational and thrilling journey.

South African style comes from the heart, from personal experiences; it sometimes necessitates hand-crafting rather than sophisticated design machinery. And these hand-crafted items are often juxtaposed with creations from other countries because, despite us living way down at the tip of Africa, we do love to travel! We also love to bring back ideas and inspiration from those countries, cleverly combining them with our home-grown things. The way they are mixed together is the true essence of South African style. Quirky, arty, creative – that's the language of our country!

I applaud also the professionals responsible for creating these homes – the architects and interior designers who have the talent to translate and implement their clients' personal tastes and styles with tact, integrity and dignity.

Similar to the philosophy I applied to my exhibitions, with this book I wanted to ensure a unique, innovative and superior standard of presentation. I have transferred this same formula from exhibition to the home. First, I felt it important to give you a sense of location, so each home featured begins with a picture of the area where the house is situated. Next, you get to enter the house, to experience how we translate our moods, reflections and feelings, shadow and light – all so much a part of a room's décor. We are individuals of varying landscapes, just like the country in which we live.

And most important for me was to find a South African photographer whom I felt could capture the true essence of our homes and our lifestyles. I wanted to avoid predictable interior shots. They needed to be photographed creatively, slightly unconventionally, so I chose to work with award-winning artist and professional photographer, Lien Botha. Sensitive and enormously gifted, she is also an eleventh-generation South African and I felt she had the sense of spirit and an understanding of the spaces I've chosen to photograph.

Beauty is in the eye of the beholder, as the saying goes, which rings just as true for this book. Some homes you will identify with, many you might aspire to – there may even be a couple you don't respond to – but hopefully, in all of them you'll admire the homeowner's originality and courage. I hope my book will contribute, albeit subliminally, to creating a positive awareness of South African design, and that it will leave you feeling inspired, and with a deep desire to explore this gorgeous country of ours with its many varied landscapes and people.

NICOLA HADFIELD

Constantia

CAPE TOWN

COUNTRY LIFE IN THE CITY

Hunter's Moon stands magnificently in the shade-dappled Constantia Valley, famous

for its majestic vistas and graceful Cape Dutch homesteads. Manicured vineyards

backed by the imposing Constantiaberg and spectacular views across to False Bay set

the scene for a charmed lifestyle.

Below the house horses roam, and owls, Egyptian geese and guinea fowl live

in the adjoining forest. So rural, yet a stone's throw from the city buzz of central

Cape Town.

The gentle sounds of a cherub
water fountain contribute
beautifully to the ambience.

The magisterial 1 000-square-metre Tuscan-inspired palazzo, Hunter's Moon, is perched precariously on the spur of a koppie in Constantia, one of Cape Town's most affluent suburbs. The owners laughingly divulged to me that over the time it took to build their home, rumours abounded in this exclusive leafy suburb that it was Mafia drug lords who were settling in … apparently made even more convincing by the choice of the dramatic yellow-ochre for the exterior! Instead, the colour was chosen to echo the surrounding clay soils, and the walls were aged to appear as if they'd been there for centuries.

The sweeping driveway is densely planted with deep purple lavender bushes and on the right is an aromatic grove of oranges beneath which, I might add, delicious wild mushrooms innocently sprout thanks to the faeries! It reminds me of parts of Italy. Just imagine the fragrant scent as you approach the front door.

The seamless tinkling of water leads you into this extraordinary entrance – a vast glass atrium where the central focus is a second water feature. The centre of the court soars upward towards a massive skylight reminiscent of the glass pyramid at the Louvre in Paris. Light floods in by day and stars twinkle through the glazed panels by night. Imagine the dramatic effect of our infamous Cape storms lashing against the glass in winter!

All the rooms, whether at ground or gallery level, lead off the atrium. The family is watched over protectively by Sam the Sheriff, fashioned of papier-mâché by Francois van Reenen.

Top: The Helen of Troy lampstand allows light to shine through her eyes. **Above:** An intriguing eclectic mix of cross-culture collectables, including wonderful Linnware pottery and turquoise milky glass. The bronze warthog appears very much at home amongst all the pretty feminine objects.

The earthy tones of the copper and gold paint give the living room a sense of drama. This is reinforced by two oversized, extremely comfortable brown suede wingbacks flanking the raised fireplace which have been treated differently, the one swathed in a hand-dyed, West African patterned fabric throw with a generous bolster cushion.

Above the fireplace is a pair of Ethiopian metal candlesticks on either side of a painting by the owner, entitled 'Magician's Table'. (Spot the strawberries, ring and locket.) The oversized turquoise vase creates vibrant colour relief and is cleverly balanced by similar sea-blues on the tablescape across the room.

A cosy, rosy room with a charming mix of antique embroidered throws from India in pinks and reds, thrown over the side table and fuchsia-pink corduroy sofa. A zebra ottoman waits for tired souls to rest their feet on its striped back.

Opposite the sofa are four family portraits. The two wingbacks used to reside at the office but were brought home and reupholstered in a pretty pink check. The owner, determined to echo the exterior house colouring, subjected the study to six coats of paint before she was convinced she had achieved the right ochrey tones.

The snow room … In this dining room of browns, creams and whites, different styles of chairs have been mixed around a chunky, waxed, brown table made of rafters salvaged from the owners' previous renovated home. Over the table hangs a locally made wrought-iron chandelier.

Mirrored screens create an interesting play of reflections and light, particularly at night in a candle-light setting. The black-and-white chalk painting is by Durban artist Pascal Chandler. An Art Nouveau light on the sideboard contrasts with the paleness of ostrich eggs and ivory elephants.

Sheets of soundproof shatterproof glass separating the kitchen from the atrium reveal the drama of the jungly view beyond whilst keeping the warm, yeasty aromas of freshly home-baked bread at bay.

The kitchen cabinets were originally cherry wood, but the owner, deciding this was too dark, bravely slapped on a coat of white paint. Marble tops add sophistication.

The honky-tonk piano was treated to a similar lick of white paint. The painting by the owner depicts herself and her children playing on their bed while holidaying in Mauritius.

Glass French doors open sensuously into the gigantic bathroom from the open-plan sitting area and bedroom of the main suite, where silk curtains of red and nicotined-cream stripes spill lavishly onto the floor. The generous shower is open, the cupboards freestanding, and a Persian rug anchors the room. The owner chose not to have tiles on the walls as this would have made the room appear too busy.

The petite owner bathing reminds me of a beautiful painting by French Impressionist Edgar Dégas.

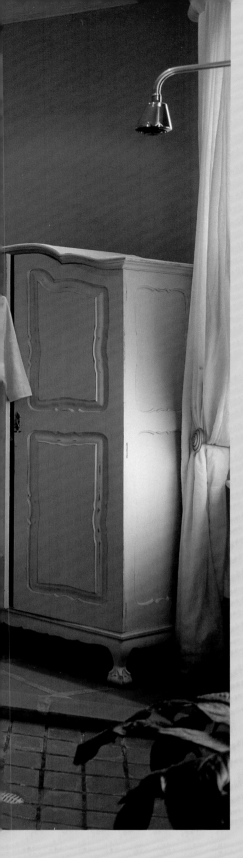

A dress in sumptuous fabric is draped across the bed in this melodramatic setting – the owner loves dressing up in richly textured medieval gowns and has all her clothes personally made for her.

There is a confident choice of patterns in this child's bedroom – black-and-white patterned curtains, dalmation spots in velvet, a riempie bench ('so our little girl can climb up onto her bed'), and brown walls … Interesting, but it works!

Stellenbosch

CAPE WINELANDS

LIVING BETWEEN OLIVE GROVES AND VINES

Stellenbosch, with its historic Cape Dutch architecture and wine-making heritage, enjoys panoramic vistas of the high Simonsberg, lush Ida's Valley and, in the distance, Table Mountain flanking False Bay. And the surrounding mountainside sometimes even reveals an occasional leopard. The fertile valley is well wooded with tall, leafy oaks, testimony to the efforts of the early farming settlers. This graceful home, too, has its oaks, standing sentinel alongside the driveway.

The long, curvaceous sweep of the brick-paved drive is lined with purple hues. Lilac mini-agapanthus and deep gentian-violet French lavender hug the edge as the driveway leads expectantly to this Cape Dutch Revival homestead. The seamless palette of purples ushering you up to the house flows, uninterrupted, to the creepers falling from the eaves of the house, heavily laden (in season) with lilac wisteria. Placed in the central water feature, potted Japanese bearded irises create an indigo-hued focal point within the generously sized courtyard. The hand-crafted teak door with its wrought-iron detailing makes an interesting first impression.

The internal courtyard is designed in the shape of a star. Picking up the theme, the bronze sculpture by Florian Wozniak, suspended above the water feature, is appropriately titled 'Star Gazer'.

Left: The farm, flanked on all sides by trellised vines and olive trees, was previously owned by passionate gardeners, whose efforts the present owner – herself green fingered – is happy to continue. Layers of texture and colour range from luminescent green to violet to the russet shades of autumn. Florian Wozniak also sculpted the seated figures (above) at the pool.

This informal entertaining space with its internal braai and pizza oven can be completely opened up on all sides to the leafy layers of the magnificent garden. The views extend to False Bay and, on clear days, even Cape Point. Crisp green apples nestle quite naturally in the carved indentation of the imbuia coffee table. Stone and white horizontal bands painted onto the wall lend a modern feel.

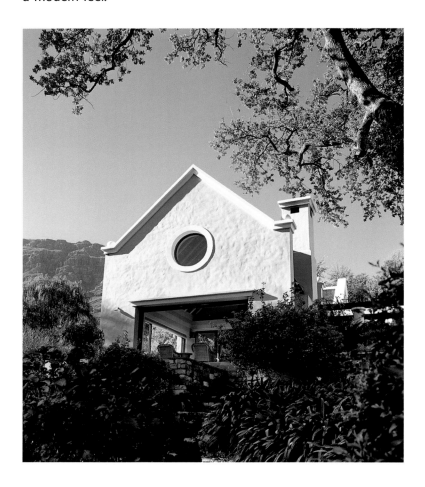

This large, formal living room comfortably carries a couple of oversized sofas, one deep aubergine, the other rich magenta. In summer, the colours make way for lighter covers. The aquamarine and tanzanite-blue silk cushions provide a striking contrast to the sofas, while the thick silk curtains remain neutral.

William Kentridge, South African artist supreme, was commissioned to create his first ever fresco and, inspired by the double-volume windows, he painted an angel, which he named 'Protector of the House'. The owners are able to communicate with the angel by means of the loudspeaker next to the typewriter.

Top: The vivid colours in this painting by the late artist-poet Maud Sumner lend authenticity to the choice of colours in the living room. **Above:** A young boy, painted by South African artist Frans Oerder, is absorbed in a traditional game played with small stones.

The owner has a passion for cooking in her cherry wood open-plan kitchen (above), using vegetables from her organically cultivated garden and her own olive oil. Solly Moses rises like clockwork at dawn each day, rain or shine, to work in the vegetable garden. He is so insistent about this that the owners have erected a makeshift light for him so that he can get down to work in those early mornings when the garden is still blanketed in darkness.

Above: Each of the ten dining room chairs, hand-painted in meticulous detail by artist Lisa Phillips, offers a historically-flavoured picturescape – all tell their own story about the Cape, from farm life and the early days of Stellenbosch to Table Mountain and Vasco da Gama rounding the Cape of Good Hope.

The large proportions of the living room across the hallway are echoed here in the dining room, where a custom-designed wrought-iron chandelier hangs dramatically above the table. On achingly cold winter evenings a sandstone fireplace takes away the chill; on balmy summer nights the sliding door, opening onto a little courtyard, filters in the breeze.

If you peer more closely at the pertly pleated tablecloths of the side tables, they are, in fact, hand-painted resin.

The courtyard wall, with its marble carving by sculptor Willem Strydom, features a leopard and the outline of the ever-present Simonsberg.

Sabi Sands

MPUMALANGA

LAND OF THE RISING SUN

This privately owned farm is tucked into the folds of a mountain that belongs to the majestic Drakensberg escarpment. The view stretches to infinity under skies that appear to have been whitewashed with giant brushstrokes and against which acacias trace their razor-sharp silhouettes. Gnarled and twisted branches create organic sculptures of nature – God's own artwork.

As the burning red sunset dips slowly out of sight, it's the perfect time to head out for early evening cocktails to toast in a diversity of animals, emerging from their siesta after the heat of the day. They warily eye one another as they make their skittish way to the watering holes, while a Scops owl calls in the distance and the smell of the earthy wild potato shrub permeates the senses.

Preferring to avoid today's overplayed ethnic ambience of an African bush lodge, the farm-loving owners' brief to the architect was to design a typical Transvaal farmhouse. The result is a home that nestles discreetly amongst the indigenous marula, jackalberry (Transvaal ebony) and leadwood trees.

Its location on the Sand River ensures coolness during the hot summers as well as expansive views along the length of the river, allowing guests to spot all kinds of wild animals. The sharp drop to the river made it necessary for the exterior decking to be constructed on raised poles.

Fine red sand from the anthills that locally abound, mixed together with the builder's secret ingredient, gives the exterior walls their rusty hue. With steely determination, the owners refused to play a role in today's global trend of wreaking devastation on our precious flora and oxygen reserves by destroying any trees.

Virtually impossible to detect near the low-lying private causeway across the river, crocodiles lie motionless, warming their bellies on the hot, flat stones. Partially submerged hippos rise up from the river to quizzically inspect visitors rumbling across their bridge. Cheeky self-appointed guardians of the farmhouse, they surreptitiously spy on those they feel are 'invading' their territory.

A pair of shy bushbuck, innocent of human presence, grazes contentedly below the circular plunge pool. The slope of the land gives one a bird's-eye view of the animal parade in the Sand River below – moving, breathing, living art offering a continually changing picturescape.

The house was built to accommodate the indigenous leadwood trees, with the deck and walkways of Australian karri wood sensitively diverted around the slender trunks. The pathway is not to be walked alone at night – there's every possibility you'll bump into a night prowler you'd prefer to avoid!

Top: A hammock has been strategically suspended under an *Albizia versicolor* for lazy afternoons. Friends can revel in the waterlife below, the birdlife above, and only occasionally are their dreams disrupted by nature's own surround-sound – the peace-shattering bark of the baboons. **Above:** The circular rim-flow pool.

Unusual papier-mâché buffalo and sable antelope trophy-heads innovatively light up the entrance through wide doors of Indonesian merbau. So absolutely perfect in this context, they provide the stylish stamp of Big Five territory, creating enormous anticipation for what lies ahead.

Running along two sides of this garden is an ultra-wide, covered walkway, supported by enormous bleached eucalyptus poles. A swallow has firmly settled in the ceiling, nesting here all year round, having decided that migration is 'for the birds'! An inner indigenous garden and a larger pool built into rock (not visible here) nestle safely within the U-shape of the house, ensuring swimming without the fear of night-time predatory visitors.

High thatched ceilings, an overhead fan and whitewashed cement floors all contribute to keeping things cool during the harsh, unrelenting days of summer. Rustic tones of the unlined linen curtains tie in with the soft, faded colours of deep, comfortable sofas. A valuable and quite extraordinary range of South African history books, selected with an intelligent, discerning eye and showing a fanatical interest in the subject, is hard to resist on a lazy afternoon.

These two original BOAC posters – entitled 'Fly to the Rhodesias by BOAC' and deeply reminiscent of pre-Independence Rhodesian days – were sensitively acquired for sentimental reasons by the owners' interior designer.

The view through the large kitchen window is ever-changing, stretching forever across the veld. Tropical green avocados, so prolific here, sit on a granite-topped central island, waiting to be whipped into a creamy, chilled lunchtime soup.

A turtle shell is ingeniously transformed into a hat rack above a yellowwood corner table carrying distinctive ceramic craftwork characterising the well-known South African Linnware range.

Nights here are chilly so the fire is lit year-round. It's a quiet time for reflecting on privileged pleasures. A leopard sometimes calls its mate and elephants snap trees in the distance. It quickly dawns on you that grazing hippo, their movements clearly audible and ominously close in the pitch-black night, are in fact directly beneath the raised deck on which you are sitting!

Soft, gauzy-white mosquito nets, held by bamboo rods suspended from the ceiling, lend the nostalgic air of a colonial bygone era. This is reinforced by the simple, whitewashed-pine, tongue-and-groove furniture and plump feather-filled eiderdowns. Covered in a locally produced leaf-imprinted cotton fabric in pale kiwi green, they echo the colours of the tender-soft leafy branches peeping through the windows.

Fireplaces feature in most rooms and, in the main bedroom, a fire is lit every evening to take the edge off the night chill. Cool summer breezes filter through the windows and billowing mosquito nets throw romantic shadows on the walls.

Low window seats give you the opportunity to sit and absorb the sweeping views – you could easily imagine an elephant's trunk or even a giraffe's long neck inquisitively popping in through the window! There's a real sense of Karen Blixen's *Out of Africa* here.

Top: The landscape painting of the farmhouse above the fireplace, by aspiring young Cape Town artist Nicholas Hadfield, was commissioned by a loyal band of friends as a thank-you to the owners for their hospitality.
Above: There's something sensual about showering in the wild outdoors, and there's a good chance you could be entertaining voyeuristic baboons.

Houghton

JOHANNESBURG

MINING MAGNATES AND MANSIONS

This gracious, established suburb, situated in an undulating landscape, has wide, tree-lined avenues crisscrossing one another in a logical, user-friendly grid. The branches of the magnificent plane trees arch high overhead, offering lots of dappled shade. As one of Johannesburg's older suburbs, it was here, in Houghton, that many of the original gold mining magnates came to settle.

This used to be a dark, gloomy home with a long, narrow passage running down the centre, characteristic of the standardised, 1950s-style homes that were once churned out, all hugely reminiscent of the 'two eyes and a nose' template on which we based our nursery school drawings in earlier days.

Conceptualising a modern version of a Transvaal 'block' house, the architect-owner gutted the building to bring in light, sensitively refurbishing the home without losing its essence and integrity. Passages were removed and the spaces converted into galleries for her collection of original artworks and artefacts inherited from the family dynasty, and ethnic pieces acquired around the world. She converted the horizontal, single-pane windows to a cottage-pane style to echo the square sandstone blocks of the house façade. Gentle, shallow steps lead down to the garden where the sloped contour accommodates two ponds, built at different levels but connected by a channel which carries water from the higher to the lower pond, ending at the focal point, the fountain. A somewhat incongruous sound in the middle of a city, but adding a rural farm-like feel, is the regular five o'clock wake-up call from the neighbour's rooster! This *is*, after all, Africa's charm!

Not wanting to lose any light penetrating the house, a wide, open patio and steel-trellis pergola were built at the front. Sweet-smelling jasmine and Boston creeper trail over the pergola, whose crisscross design mimics the lines of the terracotta floor below.

Top: There is a pure simplicity and a sense of symmetry to this still life of rolls of architectural plans and a Buddhist puppet. Natural tones of cream and burnished brown are in perfect harmony with textures of paper, wood and basketry. **Above:** A curious mix of artefacts jostle for space atop a beautiful Chinese chest.

The owner is also an avid book collector — entire walls feature books ranging in subject from architecture and travel to culinary pleasures, her special passion. She admits she has come to a point in her life where she must now barter with herself and insists that for every new book acquired she will remove one. A Maud Sumner portrait of the owner's mother presides over a collection of wooden dolls and West African baskets. Top left is Norman Catherine's artwork entitled 'Who Nose?'.

In the living room an Indian daybed converted into a coffee table carries masks of the West African Yoruba tribe. The Teke Turkoman carpet from Iraq – in the owner's opinion, the more worn the better! – is testament to a world she once belonged to, and understands

Top right: In the dining room, tilting the shutters lets in a natural flow of cool air and tempers the light, especially the harsh west afternoon sun. Despite being a curtainless home, noise is fully absorbed by the abundance of carpets. **Right:** In the entrance hall a cardboard doll bought at a fete shares space with another of Norman Catherine's works, entitled 'Who Nose The Way?', and a big-bellied Senufo fertility bird, carved from a single trunk.

The owner has expressly stayed away from traditional, commercial upholstery fabrics, choosing instead to cover furniture and cushions with Thai or Balinese sarongs or cuts of African woven cloth.

In the bathroom a procession of African wooden animals is gathered on the honed, cross-cut travertine floor. Hanging at a higher level, between two vertically proportioned windows, are a couple of original Italian Fornasetti plates, again reflecting the eclecticism of the owner's cherished collection of artefacts.

Flanked by an Irma Stern painting, this Indian four-poster bed in the main bedroom has at its foot an original kung fu bench; from it, according to the owner, the bronze African leopard watches over her at night. The Chinese temple figure standing on an inlaid wooden Dutch chest of drawers offers spiritual serenity. Mink and Swakara fur coats once belonging to the owner's late mother sat in her cupboards for years, gathering fish moths, so she has lovingly altered them into gorgeous bed throws for those long wintry nights.

The owner has a penchant for picking up unusual objects, all with their own stories and imbued with special meaning and sentimental value – she also has collections within collections! Her miscellany of animals – both real and unreal – are her family, her home a mystical sanctuary. You can't help but think of Noah's ark and the animals who came in, two by two!

Friends are often entertained on the island in the koi pond where a frogs' chorus, mandarin ducks and the gurgle of the water spouts set the tone for wonderful atmospheric dinners. They may be treated to personal favourites like chilled pink-bougainvillea borscht and roasted quail, served on rustic brown Portuguese plates that harmonise with the rough terracotta floor.

The hand-cut, finely polished Bohemian glasses lend an understated sense of sophistication to the rustic setting.

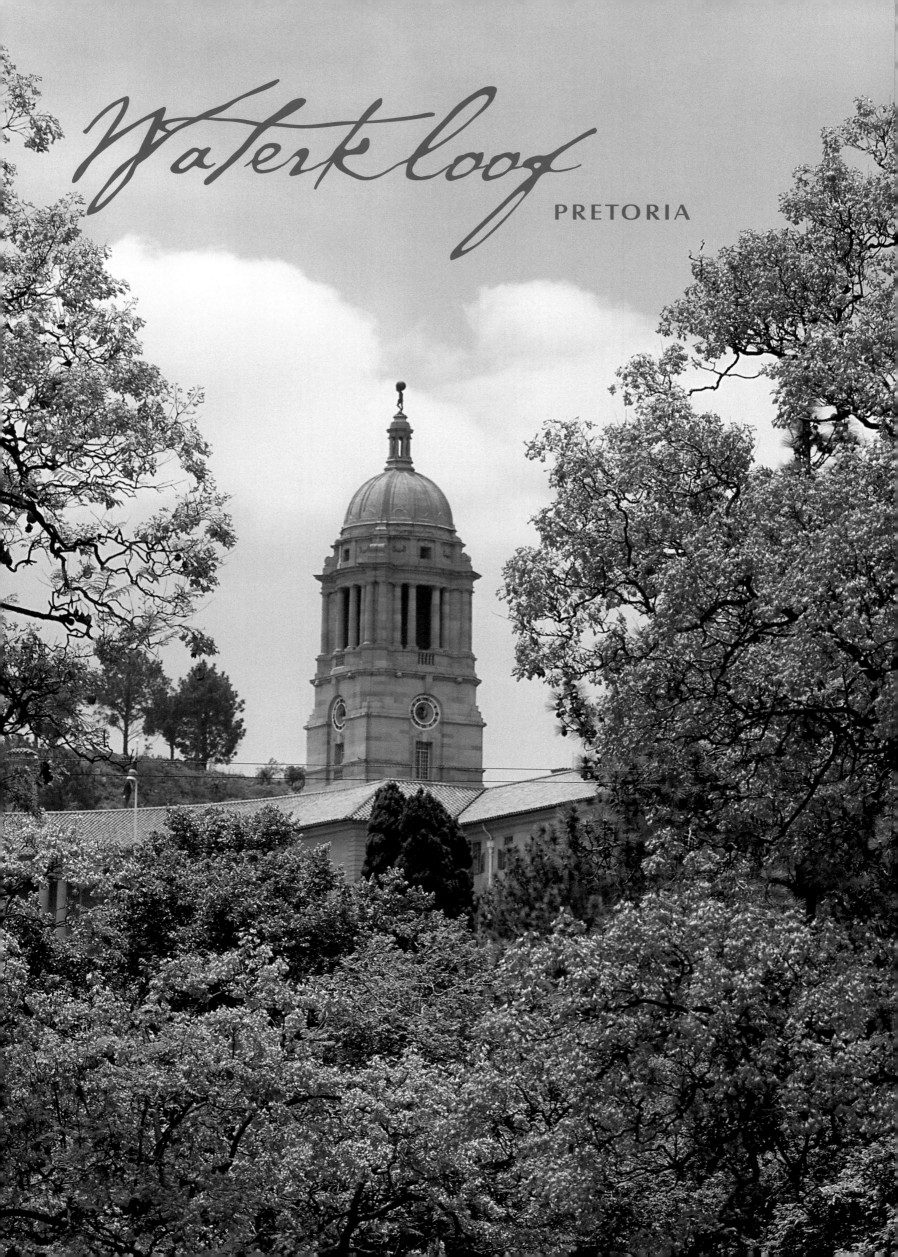

Waterkloof

PRETORIA

HOT POLITICIANS AND HADEDAS

Nelson Mandela was inaugurated as our first democratically-elected president in

1994 in this administrative capital, renowned equally for its educational facilities,

monuments and museums as for its regal ambassadorial residences. Here, the

warm, characterful Afrikaans language is juxtaposed with the foreign accents of

the embassies. In spring, expect to see wide avenues of jacarandas in full bloom

saluting one another like guards of honour in stately seamless purple rows.

The interesting decision to mix different types and sizes of stone gives the impression that the house has been added onto over time. Lesotho sandstone was painstakingly selected and chiselled before being clad to the exterior to look as if it was dry stacked. The natural clay-tiled rooftop of the lower-lying cottage creates an aesthetic and acoustic barrier to the road below.

An extraordinary contemporary take on a Free State farmhouse in a French village-inspired gated estate on the outskirts of Pretoria. Whew! Purposely designed narrow cobbled lanes invite a charming olde-worlde courteousness as cars politely make way for one another to pass, and innovative architectural features create privacy despite the closeness of the individual homes. Belying the size of its property, this cleverly proportioned house reaches skyward. Dramatically exaggerated proportions – from the extra-thick walls, deep skirtings, three-metre-high doors and windows to chunky pillars of extraordinary dimensions – demanded building materials that were locally sourced and manufactured.

The owners voluntarily landscaped the public space fronting onto their home by planting over 200 indigenous bushwillows and water-conserving sweet-thorn trees, attracting the yelling hadedas back to the area. On moonlit evenings residents can stroll around the estate, embracing the quiet after a wearying day, interrupted only by the fish jumping in the dam or the ducks calling to their mates across the waters.

A pair of French country occasional chairs, covered in hand-woven sisal, makes a statement, dwarfed as they are by the stone-clad walls.

Sandstone pillars of pregnant proportions, in Afrikaans jokingly nicknamed *boepens* (fat around the middle) columns are a trademark of the architect. The building materials are so natural that if you look carefully you'll even find the scratches of fossil remains.

The entrance, a triple-volume basilica-inspired atrium, is anchored by a five-metre-long table of Table Mountain oak. It supports an antique horse feeding-trough and, hanging above, is a hand-crafted wrought-iron chandelier. The walls are covered in *skulpie* (shell) plaster – ground seashells and glass mixed with beach sand, trucked in from the KwaZulu-Natal coast.

Dove-grey windows and folding doors of bevelled glass introduce the recurring colour theme that connects all the rooms of the house.

On the verandah overlooking manicured lawns, mock unbleached canvas drapes frame the borrowed view beyond. In summer, the view becomes lilac-edged as wisteria flowers unfurl along the wrought-iron trellis.

Above: Predinner drinks: sliced biltong, be it cured springbok, kudu or simply beef, is undoubtedly the perfect accompaniment to one of South Africa's prized plummy cabernets or chocolatey merlots! **Left:** A large landscape painting in oils by a local artist picks up the colours in the formal living room and on the shell plaster walls. Raw silk cream curtains add luxury without demanding attention, allowing the furniture and colour accents to take their cue. The metal legs of the table are hand-forged.

Maria, with her one simple earring-stud, presides over the kitchen and is our own interpretation of seventeenth-century Dutch painter Jan Vermeer's 'Girl with a Pearl Earring'. The owners chose to steer away from a normal built-in kitchen, preferring freestanding furniture, with pewter hardware giving each piece a sense of grandeur. The fridge-freezer is housed in a piece of hand-crafted furniture resembling a French armoire and its strength balances a stone fireplace on the opposite wall (not featured). The open-plan cooking arena leads on to an informal lounge, linked by the rich deep-reds and blues of the oriental carpets.

Linking the garages to the house is a sensible utility room built specifically to store the owners' most important items of sporting equipment. Golf dates needing diarising are chalked up on boards on the cupboard doors.

The geometric lines of this built-in Oregon pine wine rack make a visual statement for the owner's collection of South African wines − ready to be uncorked and savoured when occasion calls.

This *boma* or meeting place connects all living spaces and is clearly the focal point where all manner of entertaining takes place. A built-in deluxe barbecue, flanked by a wall of dark stained-wood storage cupboards, is sophisticated yet casual and hints at the preferred form of outdoor entertainment.

Despite its generous proportions, polished mahogany fittings give this bathroom a rich and intimate glow. A stand-alone Philippe Starck bath sits graciously in the middle of the room while twin mirrored basins with limestone tops and ultra-luxury hardware fittings stand at opposite ends, affording the couple personal space.

Hand-embroidered toile patterned upholstery and linens echo the dove-grey of the main bedroom's folding French doors, which open to impeccably manicured putting-green lawns.

Highly polished mahogany shutters in deep-silled windows offer simplicity and coolness, while old Oregon pine beams salvaged from a demolition site bolster the ceiling. Against the opposite wall, an eighteenth-century oak table holds the family Bible and a tablescape of blue-and-white Delft porcelain.

Parkwood

JOHANNESBURG

FROM CITY ROAR TO LEAFY ZOO

It is said that Johannesburg is the most densely treed city in the world – and luxuriant leafy Parkwood is one of this city's oldest suburbs. It is juxtaposed incongruously between the bustling city just minutes yonder and a once-forested tract that today is home to some of South Africa's wilder animals, in the nearby zoo.

When the wind blows in a certain direction, it's not uncommon to hear the deep, throaty roar of lions resonating against the highway bridges – easy to confuse with the sound of a truck's air brakes!

This old mine owner's home was transformed into a contemporary yet classical Cape Georgian homestead to achieve simplicity, symmetry and balance. It also drew inspiration from the typical courtyard of a Roman villa – a golden summer garden as you approach the front door and a silver winter garden behind it. As you enter, your feet trample the groundcover of vertical- and horizonal-patterned grasses, among them catmint, which gives off a lovely fresh scent. Wisteria frames against the walls are reminiscent of the serenity of the Magdalene College Cloisters in Oxford, and counteract and soften the bulkiness of the home.

The owners, used to the wide open spaces of country living, desired an open flow, so removed irrelevant walls and pushed out boundaries by half a metre. A long and wide hallway with beech wood floors separates the living room and dining area on either side, while custom-made meranti screens with sandblasted glass provide a subtle division that's not intrusive, but also creates some intimacy to the spaces.

Feeling uncomfortable with the ritzy slickness of lavish drapes and décor trends that quickly lose their appeal, the owners prefer to pass up on too many pictures hanging on the walls. Commenting on how easy it is to become bored with artwork, they love lots of doors and windows, which offer nature's ever-changing and scented picture. Their daughter's paintings and her black-and-white photograph (opposite, top right) are exceptions to the rule.

Above left: Off the entrance hallway the dining room is reminiscent of King Arthur with its immensely solid antique suite of English oak, inherited from a grandfather. Confidently upholstered in cranberry suede, they're juxtaposed with an earthy Zanzibari table runner of hand-dyed, pumpkin-coloured raffia beaded with cowrie shells.

A large Zen-like fireplace stacked with driftwood collected on Wild Coast summer holidays was inspired by childhood years of crackling beach bonfires. This is a real fireplace, not the 'play' type for ornamental effect!

Above and below: The lack of rails on this daring raw sandstone-and-plaster-effect stairway lends a certain purity of line as it leads skyward from the dining room to the art studio. **Right:** Work in progress in the artist's studio.

The owner spent her childhood on an estate in the heart of the KwaZulu-Natal Midlands and professes still to be a simple, nature-loving farm girl at heart. Her intellectual, artistically talented family wanted to create a sanity-restoring haven for their contemporary Jozi lifestyle, and she admits that theirs is an eclectic style.

Partial to a pared-down look and natural earthy tones and textures, the owner has adapted the credo of an international interior designer: 'When there is nothing left to take away, it is complete.'

French doors open to welcome the north-situated winter garden into the main bedroom. This silver-themed heritage garden is symmetrically terraced, with a formal stone-edged lawn, and planted with sweet-scented herbs, star jasmine, clematis and roses. Silvery hues continue in the sculptural lines of the olive, cypress and birch trees. In the cool mornings, bright barbets, weavers and thrushes busy themselves among the wild olive trees.

Rolled wooden blinds against an open sash window give the main bathroom a clean, uncluttered feel. The delightfully regal Siamese with her quintessentially South African name, Toyi-toyi, has found her favourite hot spot – a miniature internal courtyard connecting to the main bedroom.

The winter garden seen from the bedrooms. A curtain of water, metallic as liquid mercury, tapers over travertine into a seven-metre charcoal rill. Lit up at night, the musical sounds of the water help disguise the noise of traffic and the occasional jazz concert at nearby Zoo Lake. The height of the wall backing the fountain serves to hide a neighbouring crooked roof.

Above: A practical yet attractive vertical hatch between the kitchen and open, colonnaded hallway makes sure there is no sense of exclusion from people and activity going on in the rest of the house. From here you can even take a peek at the television in the family room across the hallway.

Overlooking the silvery garden, an intriguing setting for an alfresco dinner on the deep, colonnaded, cement-tiled patio is created by pairing inherited original Spode crockery with a local South African ceramist's candlesticks. The owners are great family entertainers – young people react well to the openness of this home, which is

Mouille Point

CAPE TOWN

SLICK CITY LIFE AND CRASHING WAVES

Once known as the 'Cinderella of seaside resorts, real-estate moguls now call it the Platinum Mile. Today it's a mix of Fifties Art Deco buildings interspersed with state-of-the-art highrise apartment blocks, boutique hotels, sophisticated restaurants and nightclubs. The historic lighthouse booms loud on cold misty-grey days, protectively warning passing boats and ships on their way to nearby Table Bay. But on summer evenings, the sweeping lighthouse beam spotlights the twinkling, frothy-white tips of the icy Atlantic waves.

The jet-setting owners, who travel most months of the year, wanted to create a slick city contrast to their country estate with its antiques and old natural-floral linens. Stepping out of the plush suede-clad elevator of this 'house in the sky' penthouse, a generously high, double-volume hallway welcomes you – and you could be forgiven for thinking you're entering a sophisticated New York apartment. As you reach the top of the stairs the recessed facing wall is dominated by a pair of Chinese life-size ancestral paintings.

The mix of light oak and dark *wenge* wood in the flooring was specially laid to mirror the oval shape of the ceiling and skylight above. The unusual steel balustrade with its two concentric-circle rings, inspired by a similar design spotted abroad by the owner, adds a contemporary yet Art Deco-inspired twist. To create the pair of female statues, sculptor Egon Tania melded different pieces and colours of wood together, then sculpted, polished and painted them – the aim: to achieve elegance, but with an element of naughtiness, hinted at by the leggy, boot-clad lady who conceals a gambling die in her fingers.

Above: Purposefully avoiding predictable square rooms and unnecessary doors, spaces were stylishly designed to have curving walls and ceilings with wavy bulkheads. The curves of the walls, featuring classic architraves and skirtings, gently lead you from one area to the next. The ceiling has been gold-leafed, creating light and interesting reflections in the passageway. Below this hangs a Maud Sumner painting.

The internal balcony of the library, overlooking the living room, presents an interesting architectural feature above South African artist Neil Rodger's 'Girl in Harlequin Jacket'. The painting's colours give purpose to the choice of patterns and shades in the silk cushions. The coffee table, clad in faux shagreen, supports intriguing objects collected on world travels.

To allow fluidity, there are no doors in the living areas and the long ottoman upholstered in zebra skin creates a low dividing element between the dining area and the living room.

Left: The jewel colours of French Lalique glassware, enhanced by individual uplights, make a profound statement, day or night. **Top:** The painting by Andrew Putter, in soft sepias, lends the study a suitably intellectual, business-like air. A Dylan Lewis sculpture sits on a modern leather-clad desk. **Above:** A leather console separates the seating areas. Another sculpture by close friend Dylan Lewis adorns the room.

High ceilings and a striking fox-red, leather-clad wall add drama to the dining room, giving it a ritzy, slick ambience. Clearly this room has hosted interesting, cosmopolitan guests. Behind the drawn silk curtains the city spreads out forever, it seems, transforming the night into a myriad fairylights.

Right: A dramatic entrance to the dining room from an internal conservatory. **Below:** Dual-upholstered modern chairs – imported self-patterned chenille fabric on one side, faux zebra on the other – accompany a Thirties Art Deco dining table and sideboard. Cape Town artist Arlene Amaler-Raviv painted the larger-than-life oil.

Opposite page

Top left: An elegant locally carved ebony table supports a bunch of purple lisianthus beneath an atmospheric painting entitled 'Seascape' by Iggins. **Top right:** A deep bath sits on a central platform with a skylight above it. Masculine black marble edging, itself outlined in maple wood, frames the room to dramatic effect. Large white marble floor tiles make the room appear larger. **Bottom left:** The wood-panelled dressing room – colour-coded, ordered and ready for business – leads off the bedroom and connects to the bathroom. **Bottom right:** Tilted lampshades in a guest room add a light-hearted touch.

Passageways take on a whole new meaning with swirling gold-leaf ceilings and priceless works of art displayed to maximum advantage using discreet lighting.

The owners, while on their travels, were attracted by the lines of these Balinese teak chairs, which are simple yet offer extreme comfort. They were specifically sent out from Bali to South Africa for their balcony. African rain drums act as side tables to the chairs.

Panoramic views of the vast Atlantic Ocean and across to Robben Island in the distance are a reminder of this place of great historic significance, filled with ghosts from the past. The playful, cavorting seals (left) cast in steel by the late great Robin Lewis are suspended precipitously over the pool. According to the Chinese principles of feng shui, which promote the harmonious flow of energy in the home, it is unnatural for the level of the water to be raised 'in the sky'. To counteract this, metal pots have been strategically placed along the edge of the railing lining the rim-flow pool. A cacophony of squawking seagulls often swirl above, inviting themselves in for a swim!

Saldanha Bay

CAPE WEST COAST

SIMPLICITY AND SHADES OF WHITE

In bright daylight the sea at Saldanha Bay is surreal in its blueness, making you think of digitally enhanced picture postcards. It is famed for its floating mussel beds, which feed on the plankton-rich currents of the icy Atlantic, and the small islands nearby are crowded with colonies of gannets, gulls and Cape fur seals. It takes a strong and confident individual with loads of creativity to see through the wind and meet the challenges of the arid terrain of the sixth deepest natural harbour in the world.

The idea here was to make the house look as if it had, quite literally, been dropped from the sky onto a dune. To achieve this the owner, a gardening expert, extended the planting of dune foliage right up to the edge of the extra-high walls.

Descended from a well-established family in KwaZulu-Natal where gardens were luxuriant, shaded by gracious tall oaks and overflowing with sweet-smelling roses and banks of azaleas, the owner spent much of her professional gardening career avoiding the hard sculptural lines of drought-loving succulents and proteas. In fact, she laughingly confesses that these plants were never her favourite. Here, though, she was confronted with the challenge of creating a garden in natural surroundings, using local flora (nothing else will grow out here!), and she has learnt to enjoy them.

Glimpses of the bay peeping through the windows create a sense of expectation as you enter the house. When land opposite the property became available, the owner's mother acquired it to ensure no building would ruin the ambience of her daughter's home, and there is a plaque here to her memory. To the great appreciation of the few local residents, this land has been cleared for the playing of *boules* – a friendly gesture to all the neighbours.

Above: As you approach the front entrance of the house a Zimbabwean sculpture carved out of dead wood, entitled 'The Gardener', stands in a shady patch between the sculptural wind-blown trunks of the milkwoods. **Right:** Here is a seamless meeting between deck and indigenous fynbos. After the infamous Southeaster has blown itself out, the turquoise glassy sea is warm enough for the owner to wander down and enjoy a leisurely swim.

There was no alternative but to concede to the untamable, howling Southeaster that's a part of this world; the house is built in a U-shape for protection from the wind and there are no open verandahs facing the bay.

The pair of narrow, carved doors plus ten matching casement windows, with original brass latches, were found at a demolition yard, purportedly from a historical building in Scandinavia.

Top: Small porthole windows in this double-volume space offer glimpses of the bay from upstairs. **Centre:** Tongue-and-groove doors disguise the TV to the side of the stone fireplace. A map painted by Richard Rennie sits propped up against the wall. **Above:** On deliciously long, peaceful days the owner indulges in her love for tapestry.

It's worth lying in on this original French bed to take in the breathtaking views of the bay through windows that sink to the floor. The owner fell in love with these second-hand vintage rose curtains, discovered in an antique shop in London. She determinedly lugged them all the way back to South Africa, and had them unpicked and resized for her bedroom windows.

A Lloyd loom chair and chest covered with a *boutis* (a little quilt), give the room décor the gentlest touch of colour.

Top: Absolute simplicity is given an understated hint of colour with this coral design on the white towel. **Above:** This miniature 'Springbok' basin, brought in all the way from New Zealand, was precisely the right size for the bathroom. The mirror above it was found in a junk shop.

Left: A favourite chair of sentimental value embodies the simplicity of Scandinavian design.

Top: Light natural wood and prettily beaded candleholders by well-known KwaZulu-Natal artist Jane Bedford make a simple yet effective statement. **Above:** In this very white, elegantly sparse home, the interesting detail of a door handle lends its own decorative quality.

The living area of this pared-down yet practical home is simply one large room – designed specifically for sandy feet and wet bathing suits. Screeded concrete floors, limewashed dining chairs and a few carefully chosen items all play a functional role. To temper the harsh mid-afternoon sun, a charming hand-made shell curtain, designed by a local craftswoman using rock limpets, whelks and white and black mussel shells, produces a lovely dappled light.

The house is designed to avoid the wind, and entertaining takes place on the north side, where guests can take full advantage of the views through the windows. Three custom-made windows, each lifting upward and held in place by hooks and chains, offer an innovative way to serve out of the kitchen. Crayfish harvested nearby is, naturally, a local favourite.

This painted stone doorstop, a gift from a friendly neighbour, wittily portrays the lifeblood of Saldanha's industry.

Plettenberg Bay

GARDEN ROUTE

OF PARADISE AND PANSY SHELLS

Originally christened *Bahia Formosa* ('beautiful bay') by the early Portuguese explorers, Plett's sweeping, unspoilt, whitewashed beaches and velvety-black rocky peninsulas are a summer playground and retirement haven for moneyed high-flyers. Golf courses, polo fields and luxury property developments spread out extravagantly into pristine natural surroundings.

Bird lovers and hikers explore Plett's landmark Robberg Nature Reserve with its protected fauna and flora, following the whales in the winter calving season or looking out for the shy Cape clawless otter. As the sun sets, a quiet stroll along the edge of the Indian Ocean may be interrupted by a school of dolphins passing by or a lone surfer sitting out the last set of waves before nightfall.

Constructed on a steep, rocky outcrop high above green polo fields and golf courses, this extraordinary contemporary masterpiece with nautical elements makes a profound statement, yet still responds to its location. Despite the house being positioned on a narrow 45-degree slope, the owners wanted to maximise the full potential of the expansive sea views and Plett's signature Robberg peninsula.

Visualising a stark, sculptured house with cutting-edge lines, the brief to the architect was 'lots of glass, concrete and stone'. They eventually conceded to the architect's preference for the pure effervescent whiteness of tiles to stone, which would provide a striking contrast to the deep primary colours that were envisaged for the interior decoration.

The owners also insisted that for every indigenous plant removed, one be replaced – the perfect ethos for people in the recycling business. Preferring a garden that needed little tending and could be admired rather than walked in, they interspersed the fynbos with the brightness of yellow arums, pink watsonias and orange clivias. All bloom at different times of the year, echoing the splashes of colour in the home's interior. And occasional wind in the area has made the bending mountain cabbage tree (*Kiepersol cussonia*) a perfect choice. In addition to preserving the Cape's precious water, the fynbos here has also attracted Knysna loeries, butterflies and sunbirds.

As you approach the house from above, water drizzles over shiny-white sun-splashed ceramic tiles, momentarily drawing your eyes from the sweeping seaview in front and downwards into an electric-blue internal pool.

A sense of transparency, luminosity and the continuous play of reflections amplifies the dramatic surrounding structure. When the wind does blow, you can still enjoy the great outdoors in this perfectly protected area. Lemon and lime trees have been wittily planted – easy picking for their cocktails?

Following a serious flying accident, the owner needed to exercise daily, so he decided to build on a gym for himself. In order to link the new building with the existing one, an ingenious steel-clad nautical bridge was constructed, which assisted in complying with the building laws stipulating that there may only be a single building on one site. The architect's signature portholes work well here.

Top: These original carousel horses hint at the owner's hobby, adding a playful and personal touch to the clean lines of the living room. Punchy splashes of colour have been injected here using carefully selected pieces of furniture, each a creation in itself and individually designed by international architects. **Above:** This eccentric but striking family portrait by Cape Town contemporary artist Catherine Raphael undoubtedly makes an exciting introduction at the entrance.

An interplay of volumes permits dramatic shafts of natural light through large glass openings, and both living and dining rooms occupying the central part of the house enjoy panoramic views.

Top and above: High-gloss finished units and stainless steel accessories contribute to a slick, monochromatic kitchen. Aiming for maximum flexibility, the breakfast room and kitchen occupy a single space. Kempton the Butler is a colourful character who ensures that the home doesn't take itself too seriously!

All the bedrooms revel in total privacy and discreet adjustable aluminium blinds have been installed to diffuse strong light. The cushions of the ergonomically designed sofa are pliable and can be manipulated to perfectly contour the curves of the person sitting in it. The locally crafted blue-headed agama lizard, a replica of the local Bloukop-koggelmander seen in the nearby nature reserve, also has a prime view.

Above left: Floor-to-ceiling aquamarine glass mosaic tiles create interesting reflections when wet and retain the contemporary spin that runs through the house. **Above centre:** The avant-garde thread continues into the children's play area, where strong primary colours are not out of place. **Above right:** A painting by a local Plettenberg Bay artist is propped up in the office.

Burmese teak flooring offers a sense of grounding in the home's crisp white interiors in summer and ensures a glowing warmth in winter. It also blurs the precision of the boundary between internal and external spaces. The keel-shaped ceiling adds a subtle nautical effect.

Viewed from the high perch of the central dining area, the sun softly fades beyond the rim-flow pool, which seems to hang in mid-air, and the distant curve of the sea. As if prompted, the lights of the home automation system gently rise, accompanied by music that's been perfectly programmed to match the mood.

'It appeals to my zany sense of humour to be able to control my house when sunning on the beach in Crete!' says the owner, tongue in cheek about his state-of-the-art home automation system.

Left: The spotty orange fish, made by rural craftsman Themba Masala out of a mix of sand, glue and rubber, sits confidently amongst sophisticated imported furniture. **Above:** The lighting at night emphasises the transparency of the vertical and horizontal bands of windows, punctuated by vertical frames.

The Knysna Forests

GARDEN ROUTE

VIEWS FOR AFRICA

On a fine day you get the full splendour of the rugged Outeniqua mountain range. On a *very* fine day, even the Kamanassie range in the Little Karoo can be made out, peeping over the Outeniquas 50 kilometres further. It's hard to believe this rich forested world of indigenous trees exists, tucked away behind the lagoon village and hiding yellowwood, ash, hard pear and stinkwood trees, fynbos species and wild flowers. These precious forest tracts are home to the last of the Knysna elephants, rumoured to number four, although their whereabouts are shrouded in mystery.

Because the property is on a steep incline and to honour the owner's priority to maximise the view's potential, the architect had to swing the design of the house around, necessitating careful contouring into the hillside.

O nly the rustle of the trees, brushing up against one another as they sway to the wind's tune, and the occasional birdcall of the Kynsna loerie disturb the utter peace and tranquillity of this 600-hectare stretch of land, owned by a retired textile industry CEO in partnership with like-minded neighbours.

Under the watchful eyes of the Cape eagle owls, a set of design criteria was instilled to limit the number of homes built here. A strictly-no-fences policy allows nature's children – different species of antelope, *rooikat* (caracal), honey badgers and even the puff adders – to wander freely on this seamless stretch of land.

Having spent most of his career travelling to the fabric nerve centres of the world, among them Italy and France, the owner longed one day to build his own simple, country-style Mediterranean home.

Over five years he collected late nineteenth-century doors and sash windows and, with a twinkle in his eye, told the architect: 'Here are the windows … now build the house!'

Above and centre: The courtyard, paved in concrete panels interlaced with brick trim, creates a dialogue between the two buildings making up the house. It helps to unify the garage and guestroom above it with the main house and gives a sense of containment, a particular signature of the architect.

123

Above: As the owner prefers a traditional, aged effect, a pair of custom-designed, freestanding cupboards was locally made to fit snugly on either side of the cement fireplace (not featured). It took three layers of scraping and limewashing to create the aged patina the owner appreciates so much.

Right: A 200-year-old French armoire gives the first impression of the cultural influences from which this home drew its inspiration. A light colourwashed-cement staircase leads up to two generous bedrooms. Furnishings in soft, understated pastels have been specially chosen so as not to detract from the gorgeous forested views.

The architect was briefed to create few rooms and to ensure they were voluminous, spacious and airy. Tall, vertical doors and sash windows with deep reveals keep the home cool in the balmy summer months and also offer different glimpses of the expansive view instead of a single, enormous landscape-canvas.

The dining-room table is an original worktable once used by fabric pattern-cutters. It has undergone no restoration, right down to the yard measurements, still untouched, scratched into the wood. They will constantly provide fond memories of the owner's lifetime career.

Top: The panels in this simple Oregon pine dresser were given a blue wash as a backdrop to a collection of plates and glasses in riotous colours. **Above:** The style here is resonant of a typical French country kitchen, but open the fridge, and you're sure to discover where the owner's loyalty *really* lies − in a chilled South African pinot noir/chardonnay with whiffs of cherries and citrus …

127

The covered verandah with dreamy views of the Outeniqua Mountains becomes a cool oasis on a scorching summer's day.

Above: An old, decorative fabric pattern block (detail below) sits sentimentally on the verandah shelf.

Terracotta roof tiles, three layers of corbelling and no gutters give the home its authentic French character. The stonework, of Table Mountain sandstone, was painstakingly cut to size on the property. The owner's wish for his young home to look as if it has been here for hundreds of years has certainly been achieved.

The owner has recently discovered a latent talent for painting, greatly inspired by the French Impressionists (particularly Monet). He muses: 'My garden extends for 50 kilometres … there is nothing between me and the Outeniquas!'

Above: The garages where the owner paints, with the guest suite above. Glass panes in the doors allow plenty of light to stream through. **Right:** There is no need for a gardener, as the grysbok trim the hedges. The frustration, on the other hand, lies with the porcupines, who have put an end to any bulb-growing efforts!

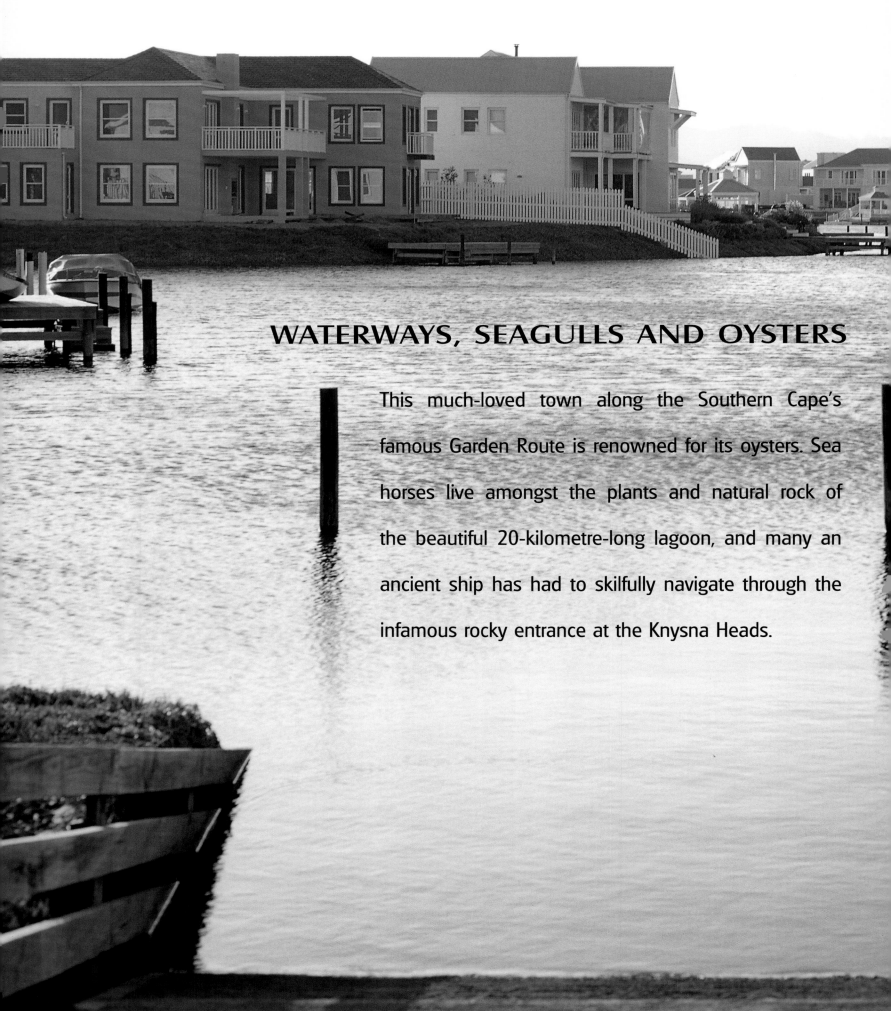

Thesen Islands

KNYSNA, GARDEN ROUTE

WATERWAYS, SEAGULLS AND OYSTERS

This much-loved town along the Southern Cape's famous Garden Route is renowned for its oysters. Sea horses live amongst the plants and natural rock of the beautiful 20-kilometre-long lagoon, and many an ancient ship has had to skilfully navigate through the infamous rocky entrance at the Knysna Heads.

This collection of little islands, linked by waterways and quaint arched bridges, is a luxury waterfront estate, with the Knysna lagoon lapping at the edge of many homeowners' gardens.

A threesome … an innovative − and delightful − rhythm of roofs, achieved by building this home as a trio of structures at different levels, creates a harmonious unit. This is emphasised by the different sizes of the roof lanterns, cutting a lovely silhouette at night.

S eeds of inspiration were sown for this house on a visit to Helsinki, hometown of the world-renowned architect, Alvar Aalto. The owners were guided by their local architect's contemporary interpretation, despite the severe design disciplines applied to the predominantly American maritime colonial houses on the island. The main aim was for their building structures not to overshadow the site, coupled with Scandinavian influences (light maple wood finishes) and a desire to embrace the best modern materials.

There is a lighthearted in-house joke that whenever the milkwood trees get to three metres, the wife of the couple feels it's time to move on … in this case, the trees have got to three-and-a-half metres. They must be here to stay!

The decked verandah overlooking the tidal salt marsh. The scene, dependent on the tide, is ever-changing − from pure marshland to a great expanse of water at spring tide. Long, diagonal views contribute to the intense feeling of spaciousness − a visual feast on a lovely sunny day.

Above left: In the central courtyard stands a magnificent sculptural fountain by world-acclaimed sculptor Willem Strydom featuring the Karoo protea *Massonia depressa,* which flowers only once a year. Willem travelled to his favourite quarry in Carrara, Italy, source of Michelangelo's marble, and shipped his marble back to Niewoudtville in the Karoo. **Above right:** A remarkable sense of open, flowing spaces is created by folding doors that open up to a wind-protected central courtyard.

A detailed knowledge of art and architecture is clearly evident and a passion for classic design reveals itself in carefully and lovingly selected original pieces, such as Mies van der Rohe's Barcelona chair positioned opposite a modern Rolf Benz two-seater in mint suede, and a pair of modern Scandinavian opaque standard lamps reminiscent of sails. The owners like to relax and read in here, turning their backs on the chilly, watery winters.

Above left: An Erwin Plaut-designed beech wood drinks cabinet is inlaid with panels by South African artist Cecil Skotnes.

Above right: Glass panels have been installed on the staircase, eliminating the need for banisters and giving a sense of fluidity and light.

A perfect example of 'less is more', this minimalist approach in the main bedroom allows the paintings and the view to be the primary focus. Two artworks, a superb Modigliani print and an original by Belgian-born South African Leon Debliguy, hang astride the owners' most important personal treasure, an artwork painted by their six-year-old grandchild. An analytical, discerning eye and meticulous attention to detail prevail throughout the house.

Far left and left: Reflecting the cool colours of the waters beyond is an understated thread of greeny-turquoise introduced subtly into the bathroom and shower, also reminding us of the hues in the bedroom to which it belongs.

Every item tells its own story – even this specially imported basin, lit from within, makes an intriguing visual statement.

The late afternoon sun casts moody shadows in a compact but workable kitchen overlooking the tidal salt marsh, reminding you that it's sundowner time and enticing you to crack open the champagne and oysters. The unusual sculptural lights are by internationally-renowned lighting expert Ingo Maurer, and are known as Ding Dong Daddy.

Centre: Marmaduke the cat presides over a serigraph by Walter Battiss.
Above: Two paintings by Margaret Vorster, from her series 'Homework', hang above the sideboard.

Stellenbosch

CAPE WINELANDS

A MOSAIC OF ICONIC SPLENDOUR

The Eerste River bypasses this home, with its borrowed backdrop of Bothma's Kop and the Stellenbosch mountains, and a historic university practically on its doorstep. At the start of the rainy season in May, the river rises rapidly, giving the owner great pleasure as university students sail past on their traditional boat rides, laughing and shrieking atop bobbing tractor-tyre tubes. The former Rag Queen considers herself fortunate to be living so close to her *Heimat*.

The architect has given the traditional Cape Dutch homestead a rebellious twist. Situated in a gated estate on the edge of the university and limited by stringent design restrictions, he has stretched the boundaries of standard architectural scales by playfully doubling the conventional size of the shutters. The owner's insistence on a double-storey home, despite the height limitations, has been cleverly overcome by extremely low-set windows.

A lighthearted element is the Virginia creeper, cut to imitate the shape of the familiar Cape Dutch gable.

Above: An iconic corner where the owner relaxes with her cup of rooibos tea. The modern Jet-master fireplace has been given the mosaic touch by the owner. **Right:** A varied and interesting life and childhood are reflected in this ex-beauty queen's eclectic collection of objects and pieces. **Far right:** One admires the owner's confidence in her individual style to carry off a madonna, Frida Kahlo and swan on an old kist. **Opposite:** A table covered with an Nguni cow-hide cloth is where the owner plans her busy daily schedule.

Since her childhood years, deeply rooted in Afrikaans tradition and spent on her family's successful cattle ranches in the Free State, the owner developed an extraordinary passion for all things related to eccentric Mexican artist Frida Kahlo with her unique style.

As she began to travel, she found herself drawn again and again to Mexico, and her home is filled with objects she collected there. They mingle comfortably with her inherited South African pieces.

A Victorian enamel bath, set on ornate bronze feet, is centrally placed in the bathroom to take advantage of the lovely berg views, the inquisitive little wagtails and gentle cooing doves – a perfect place to dream of far-flung places (perhaps as far off as Mexico?) after a long day's work.

Above: In the bedroom, an old screen found in a local décor store replaces a conventional headboard, reaffirming the owner's personal eclecticism.

Left: The mezzanine with its Gothic vaulted ceiling overlooks a curious collection of mirrors hanging in the double-volume living room below.

Insisting on having this compact kitchen slap-bang in the middle of the house, the owner had it designed open plan to the living and dining areas and painted it in strong colours to echo the leaves of the birch trees, which filter the deep, afternoon shadows through the window.

A miniature courtyard with a crayon book-coloured tiled floor leads off the kitchen and living room – the perfect, private, sunny spot to savour an aromatic mid-morning espresso and read the Sunday newspapers.

The owner loves working with her hands and found intense satisfaction laying these mosaic chips around the fountain. The odd saucer picked up in a junkyard is also inlaid whole to add its own character to the design.

Different-sized birdcages create an element of fun on the stoep wall facing the Eerste River with its prolific wild birds – no doubt breathing huge sighs of relief as they fly by!

The Berea
DURBAN

A COLONIAL CURRY POT OF CULTURES

Durban, a place of steamy summers and tropical rainfalls, leaving the air clammy. Swaying palms and banana trees, hot curries and, of course, old colonial residences. Home to an exotic mix of cultures – where Zulu tribal dances are juxtaposed with Hindu festivals, and English gentlemen's clubs still exist. Sun-seeking surfers and joggers trustingly hand their keys to the local self-appointed key keeper, anglers fish for stumpnose and grunter, and maddening Indian mynahs imitate every other bird.

Shedding the traditional heaviness of some colonial houses, this refined, deep-verandahed home – situated high above the city on The Berea – has been brought right up to date, yet still retains the graceful architecture and traditional black-and-white colour schemes so familiar to KwaZulu-Natal. The original roof, replaced with anodised aluminium and painted white, is weathering nicely to offset the crisp, clean, outside white walls. To detract from the sheer height of the concrete wall vitally important to support the steep incline of the house, a pair of channelled cement troughs, holding koi fish, was built on either side of the stone steps.

The small-sized black-and-white marble tiles – offcuts from a local factory – stretch the length of the wide entrance floor; cool, colonial, and classic. Although the original 1970s house was virtually demolished, the owners stayed with the five-metre height of the ceilings. The light fittings come from a previous home. 'I resist change,' confesses the owner, 'and I hate the thought of the new occupants turfing out my lovingly chosen things, so they come along with me!'

Top: Durban artist Pippa Pennington, a good friend of the owners, was invited to paint-technique a woven-grass paper look in light maize tones on the dining room walls. It was so beautiful, the owners joked that they risked a good friendship by asking her to continue this time-consuming effect right through to the entrance, kitchen and television area! They have remained good friends. **Above:** A strong, dramatic painting by David Thorpe, titled 'Morning Light', lends a stylish sense of continuity near the stairs that connect the bedrooms and the common spaces.

Under a picture so in keeping with the area, painted by Pippa Pennington, a lovely mix of plumped-up cushions on an off-white linen sofa create just the right feel, appropriate for reading or watching television in a space that's open to the kitchen. There's a sense of cosiness while tantalising cordon bleu aromas waft through.

Right: The clean, ordered lines of jars and surfaces of stainless steel and white marble in a custom-designed kitchen. Tongue-and-groove cupboard doors retain an informality important to this close family.

Centre right: An original ceramic art piece from KwaZulu-Natal's famed Ardmore collection, which is inspired by African animals, myths and legends.

Bottom right: The owner is an avid fisherman and when he's relaxing, can be found on the banks of a river in the lush Natal Midlands. This was an appropriate gift to him from his wife.

This refreshingly romantic room has been paint-finished in gentle smoky pinks and features English linen in a charming toile de Jouy design.

A modern Philippe Starck bath and the continuation of the toile de Jouy design on the chair sensitively link bathroom and bedroom.

Top left: A shady lunch spot at the pool to enjoy a luscious fruit salad oozing tropical mango and banana flavours. The owners have a deep love for the bush and chose to enlarge a print of a typical African scene for this wall in the pool area. Photographed in black and white and therefore appropriate for the exterior feel of the house, it was taken by another local and highly talented artist, Deborah Good. **Centre left:** Since childhood, the owner has wanted a treehouse, so much so that he owns collections of books on the subject. His is exquisitely constructed, and every family member has spent some special time up here, from midnight feasts to pyjama parties – and we're not just talking children …
Left: This old original Pietermaritzburg lamp post was discovered by the owners buried in the property grounds. As a sentimental gesture, they resurrected it, and this 'obelisk' now provides a focal point in the garden. **Right:** The black-and-white colour scheme runs through the house, from the black marble inlay that defines the edge of the cement floor to the black-painted window shutters and Morris chairs, all echoing the theme. The tickey creeper clinging tenaciously to the white tongue-and-groove ceiling has been encouraged to do so as it diffuses the glare.

Preferring the pool nearer the kitchen to fit in with a modern lifestyle, the owners filled in the original pool, which was far away at the bottom of the garden at the front of the house, and constructed a newer version at the back of the home; it also offers more privacy.

Kamberg

KWAZULU-NATAL

TASTES OF THE BERG

This lush mountain realm is the kingdom of the Zulus. Here, on the banks of the Little Mooi River, an idyllic farmhouse is tucked sensitively into the foothills of the majestic Drakensberg. Servals regularly slink by and an occasional otter and her cub can be heard barking below as they swim upstream to avoid predators. Eland, the largest antelope in Africa, also graze nearby.

This singularly unique house has been painstakingly built by the owners, brick by boulder, rock by wooden beam, without one architectural plan having been drawn up. The red-and-white candy-striped shutters, contrasting with the stony-grey walls, are old horse-stable doors.

Top: Mature yellowwoods and blackwoods envelop the house, which experiences either 'stinking hot' days, according to the owner, or stands shrouded in misty, dew-like cloud. **Centre:** The owners let each room evolve as they built their way around every rock, tree and crevice. No tree or plant was damaged during the building process. **Above:** The design of the house, precipitously elevated four times its height above the rushing Little Mooi River and cantilevered over boulders, was dictated by the lie of the land.

This 'add-on' is a little sunken room where you can lie back on wintry evenings, enjoying the spicy, peppery flavours of a good bottle of shiraz. The owners have been known to spend the night here – the middle drop can be lifted and a cushion put in place, turning it into a double bed.

In this bathroom nothing, other than a flycatcher feeding her babies peeping expectantly out of their nest, disturbs your bath routine as you lie perched to take full advantage of the nature that abounds.

170

New pine floors were lovingly sanded and re-sanded until the owners were satisfied they'd achieved the perfect pale, worn colour they wanted. On being asked about her style, the owner defines it as 'no style', preferring to allow the items in a room to evolve naturally. She admits to boring easily and loves to change things around often. Despite the hot days, a fire burns most of the time as, being on the river, the evenings are often chilly and the inviting warmth takes the edge off the cold. The owners have built a *teppanyaki* table – an iron or steel table-top grill – into an intimate nook facing the river. Here, they stir-fry meat and vegetables according to the Japanese style.

At the far end of the dining area, the owners have innovatively reinvented traditional lighting by designing their own out of culinary appliances – sieves, cake domes and colanders! Supporting these lights are old measuring chains from the Zululand sugar farm of one of the owner's parents. Four old hanging buckets salvaged from a fire station are suspended from hooks at each corner of the table, making sure the host is ever-ready to serve his guests chilled wine.

The kitchen clearly takes centre stage in the house. The owner is an acclaimed gourmet and his wife and daughters are renowned for their inimitable good taste, whether culinary or design-related. Their preference is for smoked and chargrilled food as opposed to barbecues, so their kitchen has a smoker and chargriller. With their love of old things, they found and purchased an old railway guard's-van stove and converted it to gas. Post office cubbyhole units act as kitchen cupboards and hold an assortment of cooking utensils. The kitchen bar stools are old iron tractor seats cast in bronze with plough discs as a base and gate valves as foot rests.

173

Wonderful pieces from inherited silver cutlery sets and other silver artefacts sit atop an old garden gate, which forms the tabletop in the wine cellar. Building it two metres above the swirling river and using the existing rock as walls, this has helped the wines – and the salamis and Parma hams – maintain an even temperature throughout the year. 'Instead of going olde worlde,' explain the owners, 'we chose a contemporary take with industrial metal walkways.'

Right and centre: The pantry is groaning with all sorts of delectable home-made jams and preserves. Old sepia prints have been cleverly pasted in the cottage panes to subtly hide the pantry's wares. **Bottom right:** Paintings by the owners' daughter form an artist's nook next to the pantry. Wooden slats from the doors of a demolished shed concertina closed to shut off the working space in the evenings.

Top left: A collection of family memorabilia. **Centre left:** In the main bedroom, old farm gates are converted into a headboard. **Left:** Family photographs of older generations are framed above cotton-wool and soap dishes which once were white ceramic jelly moulds and soufflé dishes.

This long, narrow room has been specially created as a dormitory for close family guests. Floor boards are charmingly painted in beige and white strips, with loads of sentimental bits arranged on them (no doubt to be moved someplace else soon, if the owner has her way).

Sandhurst

JOHANNESBURG

CYCADS IN THE CITY

The stresses of powerful business deal-making fade as you meld into the glamour and glitz of the affluent shopping malls of Johannesburg's elite northern suburbs. The green-belts of exotic trees – predominantly jacarandas – provide a harmonious backdrop that softens the city horizon, where the twinkling city lights intrude as they peek through. While wondering at the glorious wild luxuriance of the surroundings, you soon realise that this cubist architectural home is incongruously anchored by the familiar signature Sandton landmark, floating surreally above the skyline.

You could be momentarily confused, as you approach the house, that this is an exclusive wildlife retreat up north in the Okavango and not a stone's throw from the city lights. A massive man-made lake that existed 30 years ago was resealed and resuscitated, then planted with indigenous water lilies and reeds. Fish, yellow-billed ducks and a pair of pygmy geese have been introduced – and a pair of owls – all contributing to the ecology. The swimming pool flows ingeniously over the edge into a hidden trough alongside the lake, giving the impression of lake and pool being one. Indian cooking vessels and Chinese and African pots have been randomly arranged around the pool, picking up on the surrounding colours of nature. The imposing four-metre bronze statue by acclaimed artist-sculptor Beezy Baily, entitled 'Peace Man', provides serious drama yet injects a sense of lightheartedness to the rather austere cubist surrounds.

Above: The soft, gurgling sounds of water and twittering birdlife dispel any thoughts of stressful business negotiations. Life-size wooden crocodiles introduce a tactile interest whilst basking at the furthest end of the pool. **Left:** Sleek, slick and sophisticated, a white canopy chair swivels to avoid or attract sun or shade.

So passionate were the landscape architect and owners about the need for everything being introduced to be truly authentic to its natural habitat, that the garden became a mammoth challenge. The owners bought a collection of rare prehistoric-looking cycads on auction and an old riverbed was literally excavated and transported to their home to create an authentic gorge in the back garden of the house (not shown).

When the interior designer was invited to this home, he realised he had played here as a child, his memories filled with being dwarfed by purple forests of jacarandas. He was inspired to use a symphony of mauves and pale milky lilacs as his colour palette for this elegant cubist African masterpiece.

Originally designed by acclaimed architect Louis Louw, the owners decided to renovate, and his signature small windows were replaced with large French doors by the new architect. These opened up the house, allowing light in and creating a visual seamlessness between the rooms and front and back gardens — both equally important to the overall layout.

Soft, squashy velvet sofas and silk cushions in lilac and purple hues, and a delicious arrangement of purple peonies give this sunken sitting area a more formal, yet still welcoming, ambience and is ideal for intimate meetings or smaller social gatherings.

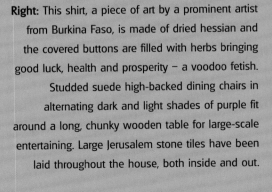

Above: A practical yet sophisticated range of outdoor furniture, made of hand-woven, waterproof fibre, has been chosen for its clean, simple form, which is non-threatening to the design of this magnificent masterpiece of a home.

Right: This shirt, a piece of art by a prominent artist from Burkina Faso, is made of dried hessian and the covered buttons are filled with herbs bringing good luck, health and prosperity – a voodoo fetish. Studded suede high-backed dining chairs in alternating dark and light shades of purple fit around a long, chunky wooden table for large-scale entertaining. Large Jerusalem stone tiles have been laid throughout the house, both inside and out.

The signature of this home's world-class interior designer is repetitions of objects, in this case, an original idea for a family TV room – a series of small cypress wood Ashanti footstools from West Africa, which replace the predictable single coffee table. His rationale was 'to each his own' – people sitting around should be able to do their own thing. Another repeat collection is the row of tin candle lamps.

A unique collection of outstanding West African tribal artefacts and masks marry well with an ancient Chinese chest.

It's quite evident that the owners have a passion for African artefacts. Electronic programming allows this baby grand piano to tinker away all day without anybody giving it any help …

Left: A streamlined, custom-designed, state-of-the-art galley kitchen with sandblasted glass cupboards.

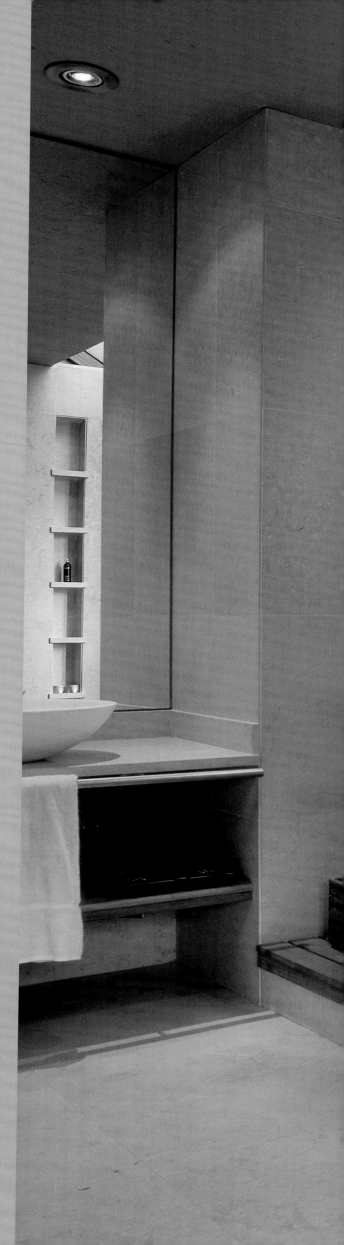

Above: A sunken lounge adjoining the main bedroom upstairs – a perfect spot for midnight reading. A hollow tree trunk to the right of the steps makes a simple yet strong sculptural statement. **Right:** This porcelain bath looks onto the solid copper roof of the owners' private sun deck. Over time the copper will oxidize and eventually take on a greeny tinge. **Below:** A quiet, contemplative, rather spiritual deck relating to the main bedroom where the tensions of the week can be cast off. The sculpture is an original Eduardo Vila. The water feature diffuses any potential sounds of the city.

Directory

PLASCON

Acknowledgments

My photographer Lien Both and I have been spoilt! I would like to thank each and every homeowner for their sunny hands of kindness, whether it was a cup of rooibos tea, a gourmet meal in the Drakensberg or in a fabulous restaurant overlooking Knysna lagoon, watching the sun set over the Knysna forest, being fed till we dropped in a home in Houghton, or a private jet ride to a game farm. It was a privilege to stay in the magnificent homes of many of the owners and experience their charm throughout our three-year journey. I have made friends with all of them and again endorse my opinion of South Africans – warm and special people. Lien and I have been truly privileged!

I'd also especially like to thank Addy Goedhart, Chez Ryder and Ueli Gostelli, Chris Fane-Harvey, Shirley and Colin Shepherd, Constance Lwana, Dawn Livesey-Goldblatt, Harry Gargan, Jane Crankshaw, Jilly Paynter, Jos Baker, Julia Meintjies, Karin Jenkins, Ken and Lisa Frew, Mariëlle Renssen, Mecky Yorke-Mitchell, Niccola Perez, Oliver and Mischelle Sinclair, Pam Golding, Kosie Jansen van Rensburg (assistant to Lien Botha in Knysna and Plettenberg Bay), Game Tracker Solly Mhlangu, and Stephen Falcke.

Thank you, Struik Publishers, especially Linda de Villiers, for having faith in my idea to put such a book together and for standing by me all these years. This time my dream is also a keepsake!

In particular I'd to thank Decorex SA, Plascon Paints, Orms and Kodak for assisting with sponsorship.

e-mail: nicola@nicolahadfield.co.za
www.nicolahadfield.com

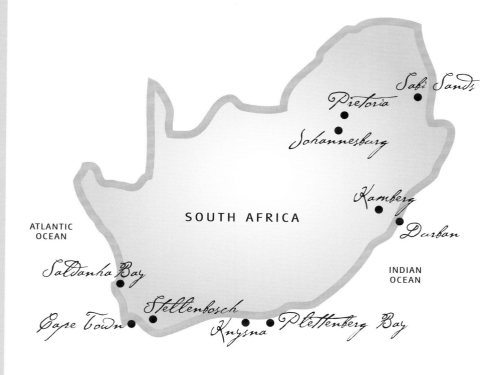

ATLANTIC OCEAN

SOUTH AFRICA

INDIAN OCEAN

Pretoria · Sabi Sands
Johannesburg
Kamberg · Durban
Saldanha Bay
Cape Town · Stellenbosch
Knysna · Plettenberg Bay

First published in 2006 by Struik Publishers
a division of New Holland Publishing (South Africa) (Pty) Ltd
www.struik.co.za

New Holland Publishing is a member of Johnnic Communications Ltd

Cornelis Struik House, 80 McKenzie Street, Cape Town 8001, South Africa
Garfield House, 86–88 Edgware Road, London W2EA, United Kingdom
14 Aquatic Drive, Frenchs Forest, NSW 2086, Australia
218 Lake Road, Northcote, Auckland, New Zealand

2 4 6 8 10 9 7 5 3

Publishing Manager: Linda de Villiers
Nicola's Editor: Mariëlle Renssen
Publishing Editor: Joy Clack
Designer: Jillian Paynter
Cover designer: Beverley Dodd
Photographer: Lien Botha
Proofreader: Irma van Wyk

Reproduction by Hirt & Carter Cape (Pty) Ltd
Printed and bound by CTP Book Printers (Pty) Ltd

ISBN 177007 261 6 (9 781770 072619)